Can You Create Online Schools?

-

Jack's Curated Business Idea

-

Jack Lookman

Could You Create Online Schools?

Jack's Curated Business Idea

Copyright © 2024 Jack Lookman Limited

All rights reserved.
No portion of this book may be reproduced in whole or in part, in any form or by any means, electronic or mechanical including photocopying, recording, or by any information storage and retrieval system, without the consent and written permission from the author.

A. ACKNOWLEDGEMENT

I remain eternally grateful to my Creator and Sustainer, for known and unknown favours, blessings, goodness and protection.

I appreciate my parents, for being my vehicle of success.

I was fortified with spiritual and academic knowledge and practices; as well as great life skills to sojourn life.

Contributions of John Tosin Adekunle and Rita Nnamani are much appreciated.

I appreciate my siblings, who've supported me directly and indirectly.

My beautiful Tolu Mayowa Tobi you are very much appreciated.

I appreciate all my Teachers, both formal and informal - Thank you very much.

To all those who've added value to me in one way or the other, I say, thank you.

To my Creator and Sustainer: Alhamdu lillahi rabbi alAAalameena.

B. DEDICATION

This piece of work is dedicated to all my family members:

My Late Dad

My Mum

My Siblings

My Children

Ire awawa ri o. (May you find the blessings that you desire)

Ire aje'n jetan (May our Creator and Sustainer grant us everlasting blessings)

Ire Gbankobi (I wish you great unexpected and unexplainable blessings).

May Allah grant us goodness in this world and the hereafter and protect us from the torment of the grave and hell fire. Ameen.

C. CONTENT

A. ACKNOWLEDGEMENT	3
B. DEDICATION	4
C. CONTENT	5
D. Preamble	7
1. Introduction	8
2. What's An Online School?	8
3. Collaboration	8
4. Funding	9
5. Research and Development	9
6. Platforms for the Online School	9
7. Profit-sharing Formula App	10
8. Marketing Plan	10
9. Monetisation Plan	11
10. Niche	12
11. Case Studies	13
12. Benefits And Opportunities	13
13. Project Plan	14
14. Business Plan	15
15. Costing	15
16. Pricing	15
17. Legalities	16
18. Sales funnel	17
19. Target Audience	19
20. Format	19
21. Language And Translations	19
22. Resources	20
23. Test And Certificate	20
24. Price Plans	21

25. Payment Plans	21
26. Payment Gateways	22
27. Team	22
28. Feedback And Conclusion	22
29. Signposts:	22
30. Disclaimer	23
31. Mission	24
32. Did you get value?	24
33. Useful compliments	25
34. Useful hashtags	26
35. Books by Jack Lookman	27
36. Some resources by Jack Lookman	27
37. Will you like to collaborate?	28
38. Will you like to be mentored by Jack Lookman?	28
39. OTHER PUBLICATIONS BY Jack Lookman Limited	28
40. About Jack Lookman	30

D. Preamble

Like they say; there's nothing new under the sun. Just variations here and there to make a difference between yesterday and today.

The concept shared in this book isn't new; however, it could benefit different individuals, organisations, communities and societies in different parts of the world.

You may call it 'sharing best practice' if you like.

I however choose to tag it as Jack's Curated Business Idea.

Have a beneficial read.

Don't forget to take notes.

Could you Create Online Schools?

This is one of Jack's Curated Business Ideas. We shall explore the necessary tools, ideas and resources you might require to create your online school.

1. Introduction

The role of education in building great countries and societies cannot be overemphasised. However, education in physical buildings, with the different overheads and logistics could prove quite expensive.

Kids from deprived homes may be unable to finance a proper education, which could have negative repercussions.

Societal value may not be optimised, there may be generational poverty, crime, etc.

In terms of entrepreneurial pursuits, the capital required to fund and maintain main stream schools may be a great stumbling block.

As a possible solution, the internet could be leveraged to to educate the populace in a more cost effective and impactful manner; hence, the inspiration for this Curated Business Idea.

2. What's An Online School?

It's more or less like a physical school. The major difference is that education is transferred via digital means.

3. Collaboration

You could collaborate with like-minds, or have your team. This could include the academics or content creators. It could also include collaborating with investors, IT personnel, etc. In some cases, the same person might play multiple roles. By collaborating you could possibly accomplish more.

4. Funding

You need to be able to fund the project. You might either fund it yourself or get investors, and come into agreement in fairly sharing the profit or loss accordingly. The Profit Sharing Formula App may be a useful tool for this purpose.

A recently popular funding option is crowdfunding, this could also be leveraged.

5. Research and Development

You need to do your research to find out if the product is of value or in demand. You don't want to waste your time, effort money and resources creating a product or service that will not be purchased.

The research shall include market research, competitor research, and maybe product research. Your research can be done online, and through the social media where you could get constructive feedback.

If indications from your research, suggest that your product is in a high demand, then you could proceed with creating your online school.

6. Platforms for the Online School

It could be on YouTube; you may have it as an unlisted video. That means it is only accessible for those with the video link.

You also have the option of making it public, with access to visitors to your Youtube channel.

You shall monetise when you hit the relevant monetisation criteria from YouTube. You could also replicate a similar process on Facebook and other social media platforms.

Alternatively, you can have a membership site whereby people pay to access your content, just like Jack's Empowerment.

Other options are podcasts and online courses.

Examples of online courses could be found at udemy.com whereas an example of a membership site is jacksempowerment.com .

7. Profit-sharing Formula App

This app should be live, hopefully in 2024. Basically, it's a way of sharing profits ethically and accordingly. Stakeholders get rewarded based on their stakes in cash or kind to the business; they get a prorated share of the profit or loss. You can leverage the Profit Sharing Formula App to do your profit sharing in a fair manner to all stakeholders.

8. Marketing Plan

You need to have a marketing plan to guide how you intend to market your product and service?

Since this is likely going to be a digital product, I'll suggest you use digital means for the advertisement and marketing.

Also, there's the potential to have a wider targeted reach at a relatively lower cost.

You could do social media marketing on different platforms. You could market through Google, Whatsapp or Bing. You could either do the marketing yourself or outsource it to suitable others.

If you wish to do it yourself, you could do research on YouTube, Facebook, Pinterest and other Social media platforms on the best way to go about it.

On the other hand, you could outsource the marketing to a paid freelancer from platforms like peopleperhour.com, where you could get good quality digital marketers.

You shall ensure that you spell out your requirements in great detail, with an agreement on the deliverables and effective Expectation Management.

That way, you shall avoid conflict and optimise your budget and resources.

Other marketing options include: referrals, print media marketing, influencer marketing, search engine optimisation, sales funnels, Affiliate Marketing, leveraging your email list, doing content marketing, doing webinars, leveraging returning clients, having evergreen content, etc.

9. Monetisation Plan

How are you going to make money?

If it's a membership site, people could actually pay to access the content? Payments shall be periodically; e.g. weekly, monthly, quarterly or annually to access the content as licensees. Once the period expires, they could either renew the licence or lose access to the content.

But if they want to purchase the content outright, they shall pay a premium.

I would strongly suggest you do it as a licence, whereby they pay monthly, quarterly or annually.

Whenever they don't require access to the content for the membership site, they could sign-off and terminate payment.

If it's going to be on social media such as YouTube or Facebook once you hit the relevant metrics, for example, with YouTube (currently 3000 watch hours and about 1000 subscribers), you should be able to monetise. Youtube also has different monetisation models. One of YouTube's monetisation models, is to place adverts on your platform from interested businesses, and when purchases are made, you get your share of the advertising cost.

I shall discuss about sales funnels later, which is an option of getting the most out of your marketed products and services.

10. Niche

There are different niches in the market place. You could decide to delve into the academia niche, for instance.

If there are subjects that students regularly struggle-with, in the University or college, you could create content around those subjects with that target audience in mind.

Your content could also revolve around other areas of interest. It could be on vocational, professional, or even life skills.

If you're not intellectually endowed, you could either employ the services of an expert and pay for the service; or you can make them collaborators in the project and then come to an agreement on profit sharing.

You therefore don't need to be an expert before you monetise.

You could also leverage the Profit Sharing Formula App, for measured and fair proportional sharing of profit or loss.

11. Case Studies

1. *Yoruba* Muslims who wish to learn Arabic, become scholars, or desire to complement their knowledge of Islam.

You could create content for that niche in Yoruba language and create the relevant curriculum.

You shall curate the content in little, understandable chunks and provide such, in text, audio and video.

The content shall be available for different levels of proficiency.

2. College students having difficulty with mathematics.

You could create useful content for them in similar mannerism. You could also include questions and answers to compliment their learning.

3.Life skills. You could create content around the marital process. Before, during and after; as well as related subject areas. Such content could benefit youths, bachelors, spinsters, spouses, divorcees, widows and widowers.

12. Benefits And Opportunities

- If you create good products, you could monetise passively for a long time.
- You could update the content as necessary to make sure it remains relevant.
- You could create wealth for yourself and generations.
- Clients could benefit from your content immensely
- The cost to your clients could be relatively low
- The content could be readily available for those who have digital devices and internet access

- By embarking on this journey, you could attract business collaborators in different endeavours
- You could leverage the process by becoming a consultant
- There could be opportunities for public speaking
- You could create content in different formats, languages and in different subjects
- You could become famous
- Opportunities could be created for you to make societal impact
- you shall be educating multitudes of people
- you could create jobs, and get people off the streets, (especially if your content is of great interest and value)
- you could make immediate and generational impact in a cost effective manner.

13. Project Plan

Before embarking on the project, you need to do your market research to confirm the project's viability. Then you need to have your team, as necessary. Your team could brainstorm on the curriculum and other matters.

You need to create a plan, linking the idea to full implementation. You need to explore pros and cons; and do relevant Strengths, weaknesses, opportunities, threats analysis.

You need to dot every i and cross every t.

You need to manage potential risks; etc.

After creating your project plan, you should follow it through, and where necessary, you could make amends to ensure that you achieve your overall aim.

14. Business Plan

This is similar to the project plan; but from a business perspective. There are also some areas of overlap.

The business plan entails how you are going to conduct the business. For example, you need to deal with marketing and branding; how you're going to make money and how much investment is needed to get the product on the market, the resources required, the return on investment, etc.

15. Costing

You need to know how much it will cost from the period of project inception till its completion, and any other costs that may be involved after the product is ready. Here in the United Kingdom, for instance, there's the GDPR (General Data Protection Regulation) which involves a bill for Content Creators. If you are in the digital space, you'll probably pay a minimum of £40.00 annually to the Information Commissioner's Office for the purpose of administering and enforcing the law.

Another cost which you need to be aware of is that of purchasing a domain name and hosting for your website.

You need to cost every element. Even marketing comes at a cost. If you decide to do the it yourself, you're going to spend time, money and effort. If you decide to outsource it, there's also a cost. Marketing is an ongoing process, and is generally regarded as the soul of every business.

You need to diligently articulate your cost elements, to avoid running your business at a loss.

16. Pricing

How are you going to price your product? If it's going to be on YouTube, and it's going to be free access, then there's probably little need to do any pricing. If multitude of people visit your Youtube channel, you could monetise therefrom. The major costs will be those of creating the content and marketing.

If you're going to have a book on Amazon, Amazon will suggest the price range. They will tell you the cost of printing. With that, you could adjust the price of the book such that you make a profit at the same time as considering your competitors' price. You need to make a judgement call between profit, affordability, competition, etc.

In the case of a membership site, one of the things I do with mine, is that I use demand and supply as a guide for my costing. For example, if it's a product, I'll leave it on the membership site for free and watch the traffic. If the traffic is five or ten people, I may decide to put a price tag of five pounds on the product. If I notice that the traffic is going to 20 or 30 people, I might increase the price accordingly.

The good thing about the digital product or membership site, is that you could alter the price as necessary.

17. Legalities

You need to protect yourself legally.
- you need to include relevant disclaimers
- you need to have a refund policy
- you need to have Terms and Conditions
- you need to abide with relevant regulations
- you need to have exit strategies for all concerned parties
- you need to indemnify yourself
- you need to articulate the Profit Sharing Formula between stakeholders

- you may require insurance as necessary
- you need to articulate conflict resolution strategies between concerned parties
- you need to protect your intellectual rights
- you need to have a contract or agreement between all concerned parties :
    - stakeholders in your business
    - between the business stakeholders and users of your products
    - between stakeholder and 3rd parties
    - between stakeholders and freelancers
    - between stakeholders, collaborators and investors
    - the agreement needs to be in writing, with witnesses
    - etc

Templates relating to the above could be found online. You may consider downloading such, and amending as necessary before usage.

Also be mindful of intellectual rights issues of such templates.

18. Sales funnel

The sales funnel is very important.

It's a funnel that you could use to multiply your profits. The great thing is that you could automate it, and possibly earn money while you sleep.

If you have single or multiple products to sell, you could leverage a sales funnel.

If it's a single product or service; you could sell this alongside products and services of 3rd parties via Affiliate Marketing, in which case, for each sale made, you get a commission.

It's good practice to sell complementary or related products and services to your own products.

For this Curated Business Idea, the sales funnel could include, 1-to-1, and 1-to-many, online tuition.

The way the sales funnel works, is that you shall initially spread your net wide, by offering free and valuable products or services to a wide range of people with the intention of capturing their interest, and email or contact details.

A percentage of these people could show further interest.

You could then incrementally market and re-market other products and services of greater value, without spamming your audience.

As an example, Jack Lookman Limited could start by offering a free ebook or online course to targeted prospects.

To access these, they'll need to share their email address.

Thereafter, an email list shall be created and updated by Jack Lookman; and then further products and services could be marketed to his prospective clients for possibly a lifetime.

It's important to note that you shall avoid spamming them, and to keep to general data protection regulations and other related regulations and laws.

With the sales funnel, you could sell additional products and services of similar, greater or lesser value to your prospects.

Even though you may start with 1 or 2 products or services, there's great potential to multiply your profit.

In summary, your product may be worth £10.00 or less, but you might make profit of over £20 to £50 per transaction.

19. Target Audience

Let's pause to consider who our target audience could be:

- these could be educated people needing niched knowledge
- it could be less educated people, seeking to better their lives
- it could be marketers, seeking products to market
- it could be students, youths, teachers, adults, artisans or professionals
- it could be those, seeking quick and effective access to valuable content
- etc

20. Format

Now, what will be the format of your online school? I suggest is that you do content in little understandable chunks. The content might be in audio, video or text, formats; or could be a combination of these. In form of texts, you can have e-books, PDFs or blogs; you could even complement these with paperbacks. You could sell these individually or as bundles, where bundles shall be sold at discounted prices.

This gives your audience choice and flexibility.

For audios and videos, these could also be in little understandable chunks.

21. Language And Translations

Depending on your targeted demographics, you could decide to create the content in one or multiple languages.

You might decide to use English as the base language, and then do translations into other languages of choice.

You need to do your research, to ensure that there's a demand for your products and services in those targeted demographics. And to ensure that you could have great return on investment as you tread such paths.

In other words, you need to make an informed business decision.

As an example, if your target audience is the less educated people in Nigeria, you may consider translations into Pidgin English, Yoruba, Hausa, Igbo, etc.

You could outsource the translations or leverage artificial intelligence tools to achieve this.

If your targeted audience is international, you may consider prioritising translations to major languages like Russian, French, Spanish, Arabic, and then continuing with other languages as necessary.

You will need to factor in these costs when doing your pricing.

22. Resources

The resources required for starting an online school include a suitable digital device, relevant skills, human resources (as necessary), an online platform (or platforms), domain name and hosting (as necessary), relevant software, funding, collaborators, a business location (this may be your home), valuable content, effective and targeted marketing, etc.

Your team could be effectively managed online to save costs.

23. Test And Certificate

Is there a need for a certificate?

Some people anticipate a certificate at the completion of a course. They see this as their receipt or validation, whereas some don't value certificates. They are more interested in the value and opportunities that could be derived from the course or courses.

I guess it's a case of different priorities.

To satisfy those who need the certificate, you could do a digital automated certificate of attendance or something similar.

If you wish to go some steps further, you could organise examinations or tests, and award certificates of merit (as necessary).

This shall however come at calculated costs.

Another option is to do mini-tests at the conclusion of each module.

Such tests could help facilitate greater understanding of the content.

24. Price Plans

If you opt for a membership site, you might want to use price plans.

There could be: Bronze Plan, Silver Plan, Gold Plan and Platinum Plan.

Each of these plans shall be progressively more expensive, and of course have progressively added value.

25. Payment Plans

There could be options of paying weekly, monthly, quarterly or yearly.

The more that is purchased at a go, the higher the discount.

26. Payment Gateways

Have different options of payment gateways. This is the means by which customers could pay, to access your content.

There are options, such as; Stripe, PayPal, Payoneer, Flutterwave, etc.

Choose a few that best suit your wallet and audience.

There are usually additional costs for these. Do your research and carry out due diligence.

27. Team

This could include; the entrepreneur, the investor, the marketer, the content creator, video editor, collaborators, freelancers, fundraisers, administrator, accountant, Profit Sharing Formula App administrator, and relevant others. You could collectively create valuable products and services and monetise.

28. Feedback And Conclusion

These are my thoughts on this Curated Business Idea. I hope you find them beneficial. If you wish to explore this further, please contact us via "Book A Chat With Jack Lookman".

Also please share this content with those that it may benefit.

29. Signposts:

Jack Lookman's Websites - jacklookmanlimited.com

Jack Lookman Limited - jacklookmanlimited.com

Jack Lookman On Social Media - jacklookmanlimited.com

Business Collaboration With Jack Lookman - jacksempowerment.com

Jack's Mentoring 101 - jacksempowerment.com

Book A Chat With Jack Lookman - jacksempowerment.com

Jack Lookman's Paperbacks - jacklookmanlimited.com

Jack Lookman's Ebooks - selar.co

Becoming Organised - jacksempowerment.com

Affiliate Marketing Course - jacksempowerment.com

Jaaloo Puzzles - Instructions - jaaloopuzzles.com

Jaaloo Puzzles - Access - games.skillz.com

Baby Jaaloo Puzzles - jaaloo.com

Jack's Curated Business Ideas - jacksempowerment.com

30. Disclaimer

We are also affiliate marketers. We promote products and services of ourselves and third parties and get monetised at no additional cost to you.

The curated business ideas on this and our other platforms are born out of creativity, experience, and exposure. You are expected to modify them to suit your needs.

Inasmuch as they are great ideas, they don't guarantee financial success.

There are many determining factors, for success to be achieved. You are expected to carry out due diligence before embarking on any entrepreneurial pursuits.

31. Mission

Our mission at Jack Lookman Limited is to empower and Inspire Generations by leveraging the internet.

32. Did you get value?

We hope that you got some value from this content, learnt 1 or 2 things, and that it stimulated your thoughts; if so, please consider sharing with others as well as sharing your comments.

If you wish to discuss this further or to embark on any of Jack's Curated Business Ideas, please, search for 'Business Collaboration With Jack Lookman' online, or visit Jack's Empowerment.

Also, you could send a short email to info@jacklookmanlimited.com and we shall respond.

You could 'Book A Chat With Jack Lookman' at jacksempowerment.com

You could get more of such content, on our different platforms on social media. You could find us on Youtube, Facebook, TikTok, LinkedIn, etc. Just do a search for Jack Lookman or search for curated business idea or Curated Business Ideas.

We've also written many books. Please search for Jack Lookman's books on the internet, or visit jacklookmanlimited.com

- You could also join Jack Lookman's community on Facebook. Search for Jack Lookman on Facebook.
- We create content

- We mentor
- We do affiliate marketing
- We do business collaborations
- And app development collaborations

- We've authored and published several books on
  - curated business ideas
  - mindset
  - poetry
  - Jaaloo Puzzles
  - Etc

- If you are interested in playing an arithmetic number game called Jaaloo Puzzles, it's very good brain exercise for children, adults, youths and the elderly. It helps with accuracy skills, mental alertness, competition skills, arithmetic and logic skills. You could find it at jaaloo.com and jaaloopuzzles.com

- Are you interested in Business Collaboration With Jack Lookman ?
- Or in Jack's Mentoring 101 ?
- If yes, search for it or them at jacksempowerment.com

33. Useful compliments

1. Jack's Empowerment - membership site - jacksempowerment.com
2. Jaaloo Puzzles - blog - jaaloopuzzles.com - jaaloo.com

3. Curated Business Ideas - blog - curatedbusinessideas.com

4. Jack Lookman Limited - blog - jacklookmanlimited.com

5. Youtube channel: Curated Business Ideas

6. Youtube channel: Jaaloo Puzzles

7. Youtube channel: Life Lessons For Teenagers

8. Facebook: Jack Lookman

9. Facebook: Curated Business Ideas

10. Facebook: Jaaloo Puzzles

11. Facebook: Life Lessons For Teenagers

12. Jack Lookman's Books

13. Business Collaboration With Jack Lookman - jacksempowerment.com

14. Jack's Mentoring 101 - jacksempowerment.com

15. Youtube video: Empowering The Less Educated

16. Facebook video: Empowering The Less Educated

17. Life Lessons For Teenagers : lifelessonsforteenagers.com

18. Book A Chat With Jack Lookman : jacksempowerment.com

19. TikTok - jacklookman4

20. LinkedIn - Olayinka Carew aka Jack Lookman

34. Useful hashtags

1. #jackscuratedbusinessidea

2. #jackscuratedbusinessideas

3. #JaalooPuzzles

4. #CuratedBusinessIdeas

5. #JackLookmanLimited

6. #ireo

7. #Irekabiti
8. #JackLookman
9. #empoweringandinspiringgenerations
10. #EmpowermentandInspiration

35. Books by Jack Lookman

Visit:

- jacklookmanlimited.com
- Internet search - Jack Lookman
- Jack Lookman's Books
- amazon.co.uk
- reputable book shops (online)

36. Some resources by Jack Lookman

- Jack's Empowerment - jacksempowerment.com
- Jaaloo Puzzles - jaaloopuzzles.com
- Jaaloo Puzzles - jaaloo.com
- Curated Business Ideas curatedbusinessideas.com
- Life Lessons For Teenagers : lifelessonsforteenagers.com
- Youtube channel: Curated Business Ideas
- Youtube channel: Life Lessons For Teenagers
- Facebook: Jack Lookman
- Facebook group: Curated Business Ideas

- Facebook group: Menteero
- Facebook group: Jaaloo Puzzles
- Facebook group: Life Lessons For Teenagers
- Etc.

37. Will you like to collaborate?

Does the Jack Lookman brand resonate with you? Will you like to collaborate? If yes, please send an email to: info@jacklookmanlimited.com

Use an appropriate subject heading and narrative.

38. Will you like to be mentored by Jack Lookman?

If yes, please send an email to: info@jacklookmanlimited.com

Use an appropriate subject heading and narrative.

39. OTHER PUBLICATIONS BY JACK LOOKMAN LIMITED

1. *Despair, Submission, Faith and Hope – Volume 1*
2. *Despair, Submission, Faith and Hope – Volume 2*
3. *Monetising Digital Book Reviews*
4. *E-Commerce For Traditional African Attires*
5. *Basic Management And Fundraising Tip For Community Groups*
6. *Monetising A Digital Library*
7. *Ajo, The App And Opportunities*
8. *Empowering Orphans, Widows and Widowers*

9. *Submission, Gratitude, Faith and Hope*

10. *Oro Ishiti- Indelible Yoruba Words - Adebanji Osanyingbemi*

11. *Eid Monetisation by Leveraging Technology*

12. *What are your thoughts? What is your mindset? - Volume 1*

13. *What are your thoughts? What is your mindset? - Volume 2*

14. *Twenty Curated Business Ideas - Volume 1*

15. *Jaaloo Puzzles - Volume 1*

16. *Jaaloo Puzzles - Volume 2*

17. *Beauty Of The Storm - Gabriel Adeola*

18. *Digital Career Guidance App*

19. *Bath Sponge Project*

20. *Community Group Monetisation*

21. *Profit Sharing Formula App*

22. *Event Discount App*

23. *Leasing Digital Tablets / Gadgets To Undergraduates*

24. *Monetising Jollof Rice*

25. *Monetising And Empowering The Nigerian Driver*

26. *Business Idea Critique*

27. *Remarkable Lessons From Mothers-In-Law - Jumoke Carew*

28. *Monetising Life Experience*

29. *Empowering The Less Educated*

30. *The Bachelors' Club*

40. About Jack Lookman

Olayinka Carew, aka Jack Lookman is the 1st of 5 Children.
He has 3 children, and an elderly mum. He is resident in the United Kingdom and is of Nigerian origin.

He studied at King's College, Lagos and University of Lagos.
He has varied life and work experiences.
He has been involved in voluntary and paid jobs.
He is dedicating the rest of his life to empowering and inspiring generations.
This is one of his legacy projects.
Though he has health challenges, he does not let that impede his mission and vision.
Even though he studied Engineering in University; his calling is so many miles away from that. He is currently an Entrepreneur, Content Creator, Affiliate Marketer, Volunteer, Business Collaborator and Mentor.

He is the Director and Owner of Jack Lookman Limited, a registered business in the United Kingdom; and their aim is to empower and inspire generations by leveraging the internet.

This is Jack Lookman signing off.

Ire o (I wish you blessings)

Ire kabiti (I wish you loads of blessings).

Printed in Great Britain
by Amazon